Where Is It?
Tana Hoban

What is the rabbit looking for? Will he find it? The youngest child will follow the explorations of Tana Hoban's marvelously appealing rabbit as he bounds from here to there and round about in his search for — something very special indeed.

With simple, rhythmic words and the immediacy of her engaging photographs, Tana Hoban leads small readers right into this young rabbit's world and proves once again that her books make favorite bedtime friends.

Tana Hoban
Where Is It?

MACMILLAN PUBLISHING CO., INC.
NEW YORK

COLLIER MACMILLAN PUBLISHERS
LONDON

Macmillan Publishing Co., Inc.
866 Third Avenue, New York, N.Y. 10022
Collier-Macmillan Canada Ltd., Toronto, Ontario

Library of Congress catalog card number: 73-8573
Printed in the United States of America

10 9 8 7 6 5 4 3 2 1

Library of Congress
Cataloging in Publication Data

Hoban, Tana.
  Where is it?
[1. Easter stories. 2. Rabbits—Fiction.
3. Stories in rhyme] I. Title.
PZ8.3.H6517Wh [E] 73-8573
ISBN 0-02-744070-2

For sweet Jeneva

I wonder...

I wonder.

Is it here?

Am I near?

Across the field

I'm on my way.

Will I
find it

today?

Not there.

Where?

Close my eyes,
count to ten.

Look around, count again.

There it is!
Behind this tree.

Something

special...

just

for

ME!